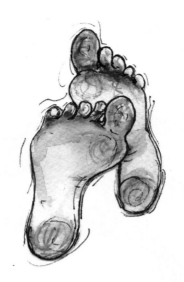

D1529762

Stinky Feet Stew

∽◦e◦e◦◦∾

By

Beth Capodanno

Best Wishes Matteo!

♡ Beth Capodanno

Copyright © 2011 Beth Capodanno
All rights reserved.

ISBN: 1456375148
ISBN-13: 9781456375140
LCCN: 2010918624

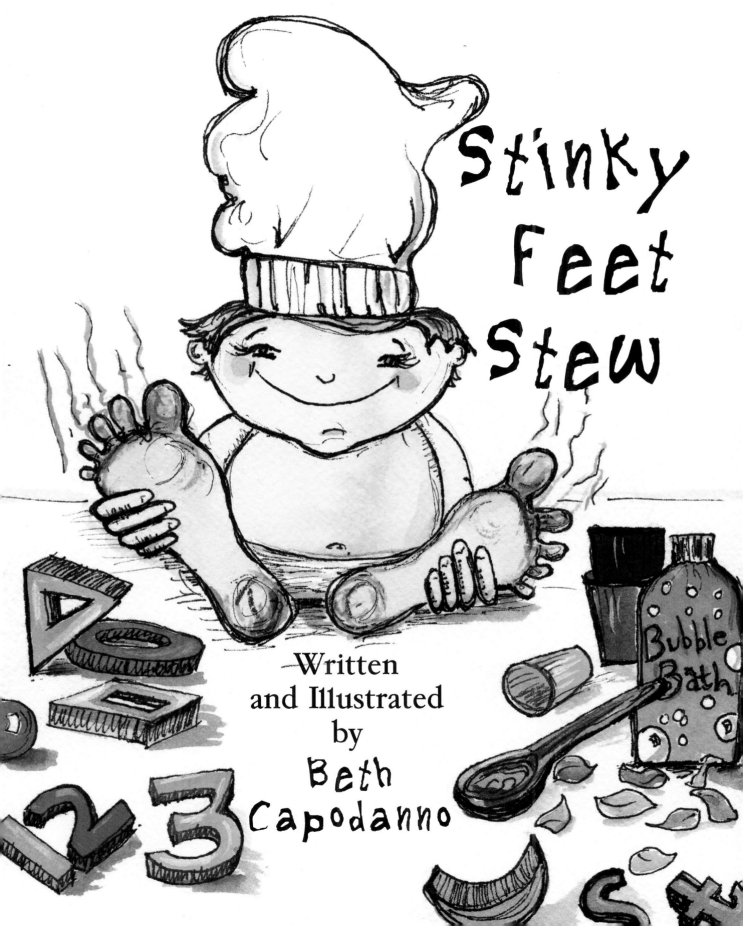

Stinky Feet Stew

Written
and Illustrated
by
Beth Capodanno

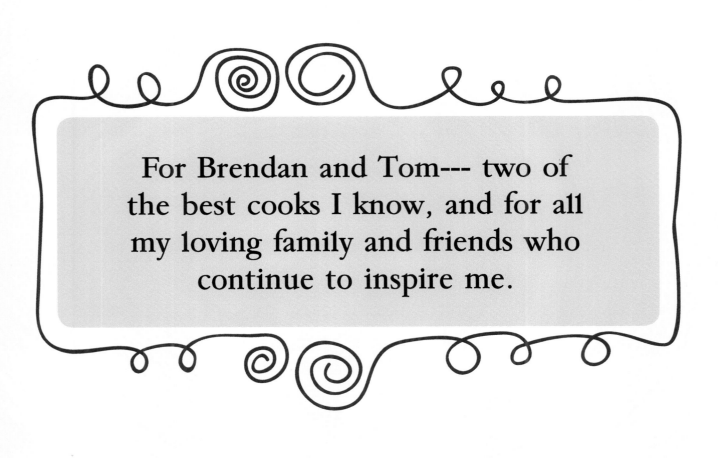

For Brendan and Tom--- two of the best cooks I know, and for all my loving family and friends who continue to inspire me.

As soon as the sun

peeks into Stew's room,

he wakes up
and makes his toy cars go
urrroooom.

He's a busy little boy,

he
always
runs
fast.

When he dances
to music he has
a real blast!

He loves to jump like a bunny
and play hide-and-seek.

meatballs
and olives
are his
favorite foods
to eat.

Stew's usually happy, except
when he has to take a bath.
But when mama smells his little
feet, he can't help but laugh.

"Pee Whoa! Those feet stink!
Yes, it is true!

Let's make a quick batch of
Stinky Feet Stew!'

Stew shakes his head no
and begins to cry,
"mama I want to go and
play outside!"

"Come on you help me--don't be so blue.
I can't make a good batch of stew with out you !"

"We'll need twenty-six letters,
three cups and a spoon,
some circles, squares, triangles,
and the little blue moon.

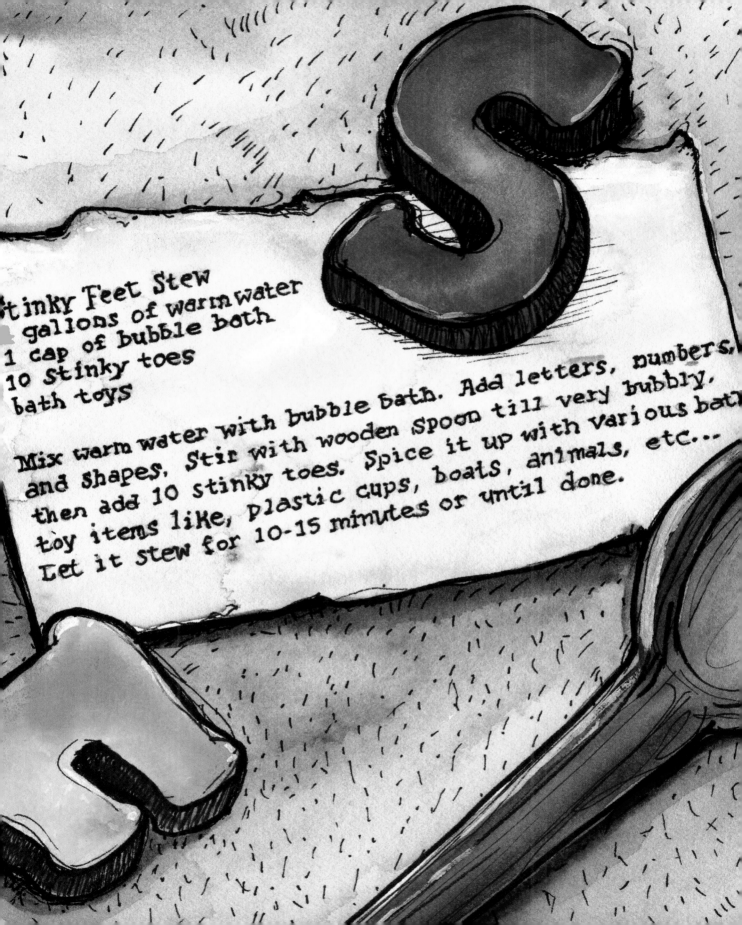

Stinky Feet Stew
  gallons of warm water
1 cap of bubble bath
10 stinky toes
bath toys

Mix warm water with bubble bath. Add letters, numbers, and shapes. Stir with wooden spoon till very bubbly, then add 10 stinky toes. Spice it up with various bath toy items like, plastic cups, boats, animals, etc... Let it stew for 10-15 minutes or until done.

Now add lots of bubbles and ten stinky toes. Our stinky feet stew will smell like a rose!"

After Stew brews
a delicious batch,
he puts on some pajamas
that don't quite match.

And mama
tucks him into
bed with his
doggie-bear.
Stew says,
"mama, it was
fun making
Stinky Feet
Stew!"
Mama says,
"I know Stinky.
Guess what---
I love you!"

Beth Capodanno lives in Rocky Point, New York with her husband Tom and their son Brendan. She's earned degrees from the Art Institute of Pittsburgh, Sufflolk County Community College, and SUNY Stony Brook. In addition to writing and making art, she is a high school art teacher.